CHARLES

VOLUME 1

BE INSPIRED BY A

PROPHET'S
ADVICE

Walk In Victory!

ISBN: 9780995878709

Cover design & text layout by
Nestto Graphics

Printed in the United State of America

Contents

SECTION II - ISSUES OF LIFE

Dedication

....

This book is dedicated to the glory of our Lord and Savior, Jesus Christ. He is our Master and our Champion. We honor our fellow Christians far and wide who have given their lives in different forms to save lives and spread the Gospel.

Special thanks go to our faithful and dedicated believers whose names God has accepted as private, but whose works are evident even now.

Lastly, to True Vine Ministries' members and partners, and my beloved wife Pastor Gifty and children: Christina, Daniel, Sarah-Jane, Isaac and Bellinia. God Bless.

Acknowledgement

Special thanks to all those who love to see God's children have peace, joy and prosperity. Also thanks to those who love to see His servants walk in integrity of their calling and able to serve God's people.

Foreword

....

This is a book that has been written from the heart of a man of God who truly cares for the harvest. I have known Apostle Charles for over two decades. He is a man of upstanding character, unwavering boldness and a big heart. From the first page of this book, you can see his heart to see the lives of people changed through the power of prayer.

He is a sound man of God who has stood many trials and tribulations due to his faith in God as well as his strong belief that prayer and confessions can change any situation that you are in. As you read this book, take the time to reflect on the advice that is presented. Meditate on the Scriptures provided and believe in the confessions as you speak them.

A Prophet's Advice is a book I believe contains the nuggets which will help to direct your life as the Holy Spirit leads the contents to your heart. It is a book that is thoughtfully written with love and care for one's journey of life. As led by the Lord to use it, I am convinced God's grace will be upon you to find solutions to every area of life contained in this book. Apostle Charles walks in love, and this book is a love match that will guide you to a fruitful and peaceful journey. As you go through each chapter of the book, I believe that the light of Christ will lead and guide you to safely possess your solution.

God is able to use any book such as this to direct one's life. I genuinely recommend this book to you. Embrace it and accept it. Let it become one of your companions, beside the Bible. You will experience the blessings of the super achievers who are the faithful and the empowered in Christ the Lord.

As it says in Romans 10:8, **"For the Word is near you, even in your mouth"**. Take courage, take heart and take the advice of the prophet for your life. For if the Word of God has brought this servant of the Lord through, it will surely propel you into your destiny.

Minister (Mrs.) Fidelia Jamesina Dove
England, United Kingdom

Introduction

....

The purpose of this book is to help those who want to navigate their way in the counsel of God. With this book you will learn to know His direction and what you should do as you journey in your path of life.

YOUR EARS WILL HEAR A WORD BEHIND YOU, "THIS IS THE WAY, WALK IN IT, WHENEVER YOU TURN TO THE RIGHT OR TO THE LEFT." – ISAIAH 30:21

Life is a journey that requires a navigator, a navigating instrument and a carrier of instructions. Many a time we are called to start life without a roadmap, even though there are many signs which tell us which way to go. We are challenged by choices and directions about which we have no experience. We have not travelled those paths before.

These choices and directions have many pitfalls, commitments and responsibilities which carry with them various consequences. As we choose, we take what comes with the choices that we make. Some will lead us astray, in pain, delay and disaster. Other choices will lead us to a fruitful and successful end, all because the road signs have coded advice, signs and information which only by either being there before are we able to know the path that we must follow

Sometimes we need the help of those who have been there before to guide us and direct us to make A smooth transition into the journey and minimize pain, heartache and sorrow. It is this direction which makes our life a success or a failure. This brings us to this book. God will always send His prophet, counsellor, angel or His servant who will say, "This is the way, follow ye in it and do not turn to the left or to the right." He may choose to grant you direct instruction from His revealed word.

The responsibility is upon us to follow the advice of God's chosen servants. We are responsible for the outcome of our own life. By virtue of co-operation with Heaven, we will be able to meet the right angel or person who will direct and help us to smoothly navigate our way to our direction and destination.

Many a time the challenges of life force us to make

quick and unplanned decisions concerning the way we must go without giving proper thoughts to the true plan and counsel of God concerning the direction of our life. Hence, we hit roadblocks which lock us down to a set path without any success and struggle and make our Christian walk difficult. God wants to bless us but we must cooperate with His voice, His leading and His guidance.

The purpose of this book is to be a companion to you on your journey. I believe it will lead you into the direction and the plan that God has set in place for you. There is a way that seems right to a person, but in the end it leads to disaster without the counsel and direction of God.

I urge you to read slowly, thoughtfully, and meditate on the word of God. Ask the Holy Spirit to teach you and lead you.

"TAKE CHARGE OF YOUR LIFE NOW AND FOLLOW THE HIGHWAY TO BE A WINNER OR IGNORE THIS ADVICE AND BE A LOSER."

LIFE
APPLICATION

1

Word Application

··

God is the foundation of all life. Nothing can happen in this life without the hand of God involved in it. Good times and bad times all involve the creation time of God's mighty hand. Most of the time we take matters into our own hands and ignore the core power which propels us towards our destiny. Walking in the Word of God is equivalent to breathing. Without breathing you would be dead. Your spirit needs the Word of God just as your body needs food. The spiritual currency for your life is prayer, just as the currency of the earth is money.

To walk in the Word is to embrace the light of Christ in your life. Through this avenue, the light of Christ will shine on your path. You will be able to see your way forward, and avoid pitfalls as they come. The Word will be your guide and your director. Failing to walk in the Word of God can be compared to failing to breathe or eat after 40 days. You will lose your life. If you don't desire to walk in the Word of God, you position your life to walk in another area which is Satan's kingdom. The Word of God is your key to success and liberty.

I now encourage you to meditate on these Bible verses:

HEBREWS 4:12:
"FOR THE WORD OF GOD IS LIVING AND ACTIVE AND SHARPER THAN ANY TWO-EDGED SWORD, AND PIERCING AS FAR AS THE DIVISION OF SOUL AND SPIRIT, OF BOTH JOINTS AND MARROW, AND ABLE TO JUDGE THE THOUGHTS AND INTENTIONS OF THE HEART."

COLOSSIANS 3:16:
"LET THE WORD OF CHRIST RICHLY DWELL WITHIN YOU, WITH ALL WISDOM TEACHING AND ADMONISHING ONE ANOTHER WITH PSALMS AND HYMNS AND SPIRITUAL SONGS, SINGING WITH THANKFULNESS IN YOUR HEARTS TO GOD."

COLOSSIANS 4:2:
"DEVOTE YOURSELVES TO PRAYER, KEEPING ALERT IN IT WITH AN ATTITUDE OF THANKSGIVING."

EPHESIANS 6:10:
"FINALLY, BE STRONG IN THE LORD AND IN THE STRENGTH OF HIS MIGHT."

LUKE 18:1:
"NOW HE WAS TELLING THEM A PARABLE TO SHOW THAT AT ALL TIMES THEY OUGHT TO PRAY AND NOT TO LOSE HEART."

PSALM 112:7, 8:
"HE WILL NOT FEAR EVIL TIDINGS; HIS HEART IS STEADFAST, TRUSTING IN THE LORD."

Confession:

Jesus is the Lord and Master over my life. I am a spirit being living in a created physical body. I am fashioned in the image of God who shared His Divine nature and attributes with me. Therefore, from now, I have the authority as vested in Christ Jesus to bring a change in my life with the help of the Holy Spirit. I confess that the blood of Jesus covers me to move and bring a trembling in my life. I am victorious to effect a change as I walk in the Word.

The word of God is my weapon and an instrument of control to effect a transformation. Therefore I denounce, based upon the word of God, every scheme and anxiety of spirit that is frustrating my plans to listen to the voice of

God and to walk in the Word. I deplore every effort of the enemy and declare I shall not be taken out in the name of Jesus. I do not fret or walk in stress or worry. I have the care of Christ over my life and I am redeemed from the curse of the law which makes me a champion. The Word of God opens avenues for me to operate successfully. My life is noble as the Word of God shelters and waters my land. It brings me into divine peace. My future is a blessing because the Word of God cleanses me and brings rest to my spirit, soul and body. I dwell in the Word which opens avenues for me to see my prayer come to pass. The Word of God is my life, my shield and my defense. I am going forward. Thank you Jesus for giving me the grace. You are the Word in my life. Amen.

2
Being
God-Centered

....

We are a spirit-being, having soul and living in a physical body. Your spirit is the candle of God. God is guiding your spirit. Without the guide you will have no light. The traffic light guides you when to go, when to be ready to stop and when to stop. Being God-minded is to have a personal relationship with the Father who has power and authority over every circumstance. Whoever you submit your mind to controls you. If you submit your mind to what is filthy, the spirit of filth will control you.

The Holy Spirit gives direction and brings illumination to your mind. To be God-minded is to be led by the Holy Spirit with an inward witness and outward witness for Jesus, to die to your understanding, to be enlightened, and strengthened and empowered by the Holy Spirit's wisdom. Then God's wisdom will flow through your inward path and you will have an unction of the leadership of the Holy Spirit to discern good times and bad. Your focus will be on the direction in which God is leading you. You will not be swayed by any other power. You are God-minded and God-centered. You will become God-conscious. Your spirit will hear His voice, and you will obey His instructions.

I now encourage you to meditate on these Bible verses:

JAMES 1:22:
"BUT PROVE YOURSELVES DOERS OF THE WORD, AND NOT MERELY HEARERS WHO DELUDE THEMSELVES."

JOSHUA 1:8:
"THIS BOOK OF THE LAW SHALL NOT DEPART FROM YOUR MOUTH, BUT YOU SHALL MEDITATE ON IT DAY AND NIGHT, SO THAT YOU MAY BE CAREFUL TO DO

ACCORDING TO ALL THAT IS WRITTEN IN IT; FOR THEN YOU WILL MAKE YOUR WAY PROSPEROUS, AND THEN YOU WILL HAVE SUCCESS."

EPHESIANS 5:18:

"AND DO NOT GET DRUNK WITH WINE, FOR THAT IS DISSIPATION, BUT BE FILLED WITH THE SPIRIT."

ISAIAH 48:17:

"THUS SAYS THE LORD, YOUR REDEEMER, THE HOLY ONE OF ISRAEL, I AM THE LORD YOUR GOD, WHO TEACHES YOU TO PROFIT, WHO LEADS YOU IN THE WAY YOU SHOULD GO."

JOHN 7:37-39:

"NOW ON THE LAST DAY, THE GREAT DAY OF THE FEAST, JESUS STOOD AND CRIED OUT, SAYING, IF ANYONE IS THIRSTY, LET HIM COME TO ME AND DRINK. HE WHO BELIEVES IN ME, AS THE SCRIPTURE SAID, FROM HIS INNERMOST BEING WILL FLOW RIVERS OF LIVING WATER. BUT THIS HE SPOKE OF THE SPIRIT, WHOM THOSE WHO BELIEVED IN HIM WERE TO RECEIVE; FOR THE SPIRIT WAS NOT YET GIVEN, BECAUSE JESUS WAS NOT YET GLORIFIED."

JOB 38:36:

"WHO HAS PUT WISDOM IN THE INNERMOST BEING OR GIVEN UNDERSTANDING TO THE MIND?"

Confession:

I am a tool of God, born of God, led by the Holy Spirit. My Life-force is alert, my soul is receptive to the voice of God and I have a personal, eternal relationship with Christ. The mind of Christ dwells within me. I and the Lord are one in unity, spirit, soul and body. I walk in spirit consciousness of the Holy Spirit's presence in my life. The light of Christ sparkles in my mind with such revelation and edifying power that, darkness has no place in me. God has brought me out of gloom into His amazing light.

I am designed and formed to think like Christ. My human spirit is under subjugation, and my flesh has no control over me. For the concentration of Christ power abides richly within me. I think straight to carry out my plans and purposes which are in agreement with the mind of Christ. I walk in the wisdom and counsel of God. Therefore I am directed by Christ, walking in victory through Christ' leadership. I am absorbed by the radiance of Christ who is the Lord and Master over my life.

The Holy Spirit works in me, lives in me and is over me. We are united in Christ Jesus therefore I succeed and overcome all my problems. Christ-mindedness brings under subjection all obstacles that stand in my way. I always overcome all of my problems because Christ in me brings hope to overcome all. "I can do all things through Him who strengthens me" (Philippians 4:13). I am victorious and I give God praise. Amen.

"YOU WILL NOT BE SWAYED BY ANY OTHER POWER. YOU ARE GOD-MINDED AND GOD-CENTERED. YOU WILL BECOME GOD-CONSCIOUS. YOUR SPIRIT WILL HEAR HIS VOICE, AND YOU WILL OBEY HIS INSTRUCTIONS."

3
Celebrate
The Lord

....

To be happy in life is a course that all living persons must pursue. For only the dead cannot rejoice in life. While you have life, you must rejoice. For somebody desires to be like you, even though it appears that according to your gospel, your destiny and life are appalling and terrible. To rejoice in God is to have a life where God is the center of happiness, contentment and celebration. When you refuse to walk with God and you embrace your own idea and wisdom which is not in accordance with God's way of doing things, you will face circumstances, situations and conditions which are too challenging for you to comprehend. You cannot therefore enjoy happiness.

God is the ultimate source of all joy and peace. Running away from God is like running away from your breathe: you will die even though you have flesh on your body. To rejoice in God is to celebrate His presence and His countenance will resurrect your Spirit. Joy will flow through your inner-most being. Doors will be opened and your health will receive life. Your environment will be touched and you will know victory, in the name of Jesus. You will understand that Satan has no power when you are walking in the joy of the Lord. Your strength will increase and multiply with the peace of the Holy Spirit.

I now encourage you to meditate on these Bible verses:

PSALM 118:24:
"THIS IS THE DAY WHICH THE LORD HAS MADE; LET US REJOICE AND BE GLAD IN IT."

PROVERBS 15:30:
"BRIGHT EYES GLADDEN THE HEART; GOOD NEWS PUTS FAT ON THE BONES."

JAMES 1:2:
"CONSIDER IT ALL JOY, MY BRETHREN, WHEN YOU ENCOUNTER VARIOUS TRIALS."

PHILIPPIANS 4:8:
"FINALLY, BRETHREN, WHATEVER IS TRUE, WHATEVER IS HONORABLE, WHATEVER IS RIGHT, WHATEVER IS PURE, WHATEVER IS LOVELY, WHATEVER IS OF GOOD REPUTE, IF THERE IS ANY EXCELLENCE AND IF ANYTHING, WORTHY OF PRAISE, DWELL ON THESE THINGS."

EPHESIANS 6:10:
"FINALLY, BE STRONG IN THE LORD AND IN THE STRENGTH, OF HIS MIGHT."

Confession:

I give God praise because He strengthens my hands to walk in victory and rejoice at the expense of all my enemies in the name of Jesus. I am walking under the umbrella of God's umbrella and favor and I hear the sound of celebration. The holy angels are singing my name before God. I rejoice knowing that my back is covered by God's almighty hand and my front is shielded by His grace, favor and mercy. I am walking in victory knowing that I am called the blessed of the Lord.

The glory of God rules and reigns over my life. I am victorious and the sound of Glory from the throne of Heaven pours over my family, my children and my career path. The joy of the Lord has become my eternal strength to prevail against all circumstances. The spirit of failure and struggle has been taken over by the joy of the Lord. I rejoice knowing that I am victorious and a channel of God's grace and mercy. The glory of God broods over my life. Amen.

"TO REJOICE IN GOD IS TO CELEBRATE HIS PRESENCE AND HIS COUNTENANCE WILL RESURRECT YOUR SPIRIT. JOY WILL FLOW THROUGH YOUR INNER-MOST BEING."

4

To Embrace God's Wisdom

....

To walk in God's wisdom is to depend and draw life from His Word; to be guided by His instruction, direction and leadership. There is much counsel, advice and suggestions from every corner of the world. Your life depends on receiving the right nutrients to be able to live your life to the full. Without God's wisdom, you will lose your way. The wisdom of the world will not be sufficient to win the race of life.

God knows best and in His wisdom are solutions and peace. Running with the wisdom of God guarantees success and victory. Any other counsel, advice or suggestions is not concrete to fully guarantee your success in life. When you walk in the wisdom of God, you will be able to build, gather and multiply securely for the next generation, knowing that God is the author and finisher of your faith.

I now encourage you to meditate on these Bible verses:

JOHN 10:5:
"A STRANGER THEY SIMPLY WILL NOT FOLLOW, BUT WILL FLEE FROM HIM, BECAUSE THEY DO NOT KNOW THE VOICE OF STRANGERS."

COLOSSIANS 4:12:
"EPAPHRAS, WHO IS ONE OF YOUR NUMBER, A BOND SLAVE OF JESUS CHRIST, SENDS YOU HIS GREETINGS, ALWAYS LABORING EARNESTLY FOR YOU IN HIS PRAYERS, THAT YOU MAY STAND PERFECT AND FULLY ASSURED IN ALL THE WILL OF GOD."

ACTS 22:14:
"AND HE SAID, 'THE GOD OF OUR FATHERS HAS APPOINTED YOU TO KNOW HIS WILL AND TO SEE

THE RIGHTEOUS ONE AND TO HEAR AN UTTERANCE
FROM HIS MOUTH."

JAMES 1:5-8:
"BUT IF ANY OF YOU LACKS WISDOM, LET HIM ASK OF
GOD, WHO GIVES TO ALL GENEROUSLY AND WITHOUT
REPROACH, AND IT WILL BE GIVEN TO HIM. BUT HE
MUST ASK IN FAITH WITHOUT ANY DOUBTING, FOR
THE ONE WHO DOUBTS IS LIKE THE SURF OF THE
SEA, DRIVEN AND TOSSED BY THE WIND. FOR THAT
MAN OUGHT NOT TO EXPECT THAT HE WILL RECEIVE
ANYTHING FROM THE LORD, BEING A DOUBLE-
MINDED MAN, UNSTABLE IN ALL HIS WAYS."

HEBREWS 4:10:
"FOR THE ONE WHO HAS ENTERED HIS REST HAS
HIMSELF ALSO RESTED FROM HIS WORKS, AS GOD
DID FROM HIS."

Confession:

*I am walking in wisdom, shielded by the wisdom of God.
I am covered by the oracle of God's grace and favor. The
wisdom of God energizes my environment. It causes me to
make decisions that are wise. It leads me to walk in the
overflow of God's eternal wisdom. All things turn around
to my favor because I hear the voice of God concerning
my decision making. The wind of God's breath creates an
avalanche of God's awesome wisdom and insight which allow
me to make decisions that bring prosperity and financial
blessings. I am highly favored because the wisdom of God*

operates in me, around me, beside me, over me and ahead of me.

The wisdom of God ensures my destiny to celebrate. I am celebrated of God! The angels of God sing a song of my name before the throne of God. My destiny is based on the wisdom of God, therefore all conditions turn to my favor. I make wise decisions that change the river of failure into the river of joy. My foundation is based on the wisdom of God. Therefore I am a conqueror, a winner and a terror to all my enemies. I am an instrument of God's grace who directs my destiny.

5

Love Walk

....

God is love. You must walk in love because you are the creation of God. Without love, chaos and confusion will always crown your life. Love covers a multitude of sin and love brings peace and joy. Love transforms confusion into an atmosphere of peace.

Walking in love will bring prosperity and open doors because Heaven will create an avenue for others to welcome you and accept you. Thereby, you will multiply and increase in all your endeavors in this journey of life. Failing to walk in love is to plant a seed of chaos and a heart of bitterness. These will attract curses, frustration and difficulty. Walking in love always triumphs over evil. Make up your mind to walk in love and conquer your fears. The Universe is built on love.

I now encourage you to meditate on these Bible verses:

ROMANS 5:5:
"AND HOPE DOES NOT DISAPPOINT, BECAUSE THE LOVE OF GOD HAS BEEN POURED OUT WITHIN OUR HEARTS THROUGH THE HOLY SPIRIT WHO WAS GIVEN TO US."

1 JOHN 2:5:
"BUT WHOEVER KEEPS HIS WORD, IN HIM THE LOVE OF GOD HAS TRULY BEEN PERFECTED. BY THIS WE KNOW THAT WE ARE IN HIM."

ROMANS 12:14:
"BLESS THOSE WHO PERSECUTE YOU; BLESS AND DO NOT CURSE."

MATTHEW 5:44:
"BUT I SAY TO YOU, LOVE YOUR ENEMIES AND PRAY FOR THOSE WHO PERSECUTE YOU."

PHILIPPIANS 1:9-11:
"AND THIS I PRAY, THAT YOUR LOVE MAY ABOUND

STILL MORE AND MORE IN REAL KNOWLEDGE AND ALL DISCERNMENT, SO THAT YOU MAY APPROVE THE THINGS THAT ARE EXCELLENT, IN ORDER TO BE SINCERE AND BLAMELESS UNTIL THE DAY OF CHRIST; HAVING BEEN FILLED WITH THE FRUIT OF RIGHTEOUSNESS WHICH COMES THROUGH JESUS CHRIST, TO THE GLORY AND PRAISE OF GOD."

EPHESIANS 3:17:
"SO THAT CHRIST MAY DWELL IN YOUR HEARTS THROUGH FAITH; AND THAT YOU, BEING ROOTED AND GROUNDED IN LOVE."

Confession:

I thank you Father God that your love which covers me is bringing me into freedom and peace and I am growing in your affection to overcome all my circumstances. I am walking in love and therefore I reap the benefits of long life and health, peace and joy. The Lord is loving me with His grace and favor, making me walk in my higher places of joy and harmony. My life is covered with the love of God and therefore blessings and supernatural favor overflow into my destiny. I am hiking in the love of God, creating an environment of the sweet fragrance of his blessings. The author of His graces showers me to breathe and live in comfort. I breathe in the love of God to know the direction of my life and to run the race to finish triumphantly. The love of God quickens my mortal body to walk in wellbeing. My children's children are touched with the love of God, waking them up from sleep and despair, bringing them into God's supernatural grace and kindness. I am walking in the love of God and all those who come into my sphere. I carry the influence of God's grace and love to my world. I am a channel and a distributor of God's love to the hurting world around me. I pray that many will come to love God through seeing the love of God over my life. I am supernaturally positioned to dispense the love of God to my friends, family, colleagues and neighbors. I declare the Love of God reigns and rules over the wind blowing around my life. I love You Father, I love you Son and I love you Holy Spirit!

"WALKING IN LOVE WILL BRING PROSPERITY AND OPEN DOORS BECAUSE HEAVEN WILL CREATE AN AVENUE FOR OTHERS TO WELCOME YOU AND ACCEPT YOU."

6
Forgiveness

....

Walking in forgiveness is to release the pain of yesterday and the sorrow of your life's events into the hands of God who is the judge of all, and the master of all judges. Letting go of all bitterness, resentment, envy, strife and unkindness in any shape or form will destroy the power of the evil, and open the door for God's blessings and mercy to follow your life.

You will not be harboring the painful

situation as you go along in life. Each act of unforgiveable adds an untold weight unto your health and your life. Life is too good and joyful to carry this unnecessary bitterness. You must purpose to walk in love, seek peace and live in harmony. If you choose to walk in forgiveness your Father in Heaven will also forgive you. His blessing will not fall short on your path.

Your prayers will not be hindered. God`s grace will always be made available to you. Carrying unforgiveness goes against the Lord's will and prayer, and breeds cancer and unnecessary health problems.

I now encourage you to meditate on these Bible verses:

ROMANS 12:16-18:
"BE OF THE SAME MIND TOWARD ONE ANOTHER; DO NOT BE HAUGHTY IN MIND, BUT ASSOCIATE WITH THE LOWLY. DO NOT BE WISE IN YOUR OWN ESTIMATION. NEVER PAY BACK EVIL FOR EVIL TO ANYONE. RESPECT WHAT IS RIGHT IN THE SIGHT OF ALL MEN. IF POSSIBLE, SO FAR AS IT DEPENDS ON YOU, BE AT PEACE WITH ALL MEN."

EPHESIANS 4:31:
"LET ALL BITTERNESS AND WRATH AND ANGER AND CLAMOR AND SLANDER BE PUT AWAY FROM YOU, ALONG WITH ALL MALICE."

EPHESIANS 4:27:
"AND DO NOT GIVE THE DEVIL AN OPPORTUNITY."

MARK 11:25:
"WHENEVER YOU STAND PRAYING, FORGIVE, IF YOU HAVE ANYTHING AGAINST ANYONE, SO THAT YOUR FATHER WHO IS IN HEAVEN WILL ALSO FORGIVE YOU YOUR TRANSGRESSIONS."

COLOSSIANS 1:10:
"SO THAT YOU WILL WALK IN A MANNER WORTHY OF THE LORD, TO PLEASE HIM IN ALL RESPECTS, BEARING FRUIT IN EVERY GOOD WORK AND INCREASING IN THE KNOWLEDGE OF GOD."

Confession:

Father God, I forgive all those who crossed my path in life and contributed in any form or shape to my pain and suffering. I release them from my heart and I set them free to go forward in life. May God bless all those who by virtue of my connection hurt me and set me back. May God bless all my enemies and let them go forth and enjoy their life as I experience God's released blessings.

"YOU MUST PURPOSE TO WALK IN LOVE, SEEK PEACE AND LIVE IN HARMONY. IF YOU CHOOSE TO WALK IN FORGIVENESS YOUR FATHER IN HEAVEN WILL ALSO FORGIVE YOU. HIS BLESSING WILL NOT FALL SHORT ON YOUR PATH. YOUR PRAYERS WILL NOT BE HINDERED.

7

The Fruit Of
What You Say

....

A blind man cannot see where he is going without a helping aid. Life is such that words carry weight and power. It will build you up or destroy you. It will open doors for you and lift you up to higher ground if your words are edifying, encouraging and comforting. Refusing to take notice of your words and speaking incautiously – without thought and care for the effect on others – will breed trouble and chaos. Watching what you say will create an atmosphere for you to avoid unnecessary confrontation and wrath from others. Say what is edifying and encouraging and see others smile and peace come upon you.

Positive words spoken in love will always create an atmosphere of celebration and health. We sometimes have to speak our mind. But we must use wisdom and tact as words carry power, have life, and spirit. God requires us to speak in love, with care and attention for the feelings of others. What you say matters, but speak with love, care and in the appropriate time and circumstance.

I now encourage you to meditate on these Bible verses:

EPHESIANS 5:4:
"AND THERE MUST BE NO FILTHINESS AND SILLY TALK, OR COARSE JESTING, WHICH ARE NOT FITTING, BUT RATHER GIVING OF THANKS."

JAMES 3:6:
"AND THE TONGUE IS A FIRE, THE VERY WORLD OF INIQUITY; THE TONGUE IS SET AMONG OUR MEMBERS AS THAT WHICH DEFILES THE ENTIRE BODY, AND SETS ON FIRE THE COURSE OF OUR LIFE, AND IS SET ON FIRE BY HELL."

JAMES 1:6:

"BUT HE MUST ASK IN FAITH WITHOUT ANY DOUBTING, FOR THE ONE WHO DOUBTS IS LIKE THE SURF OF THE SEA, DRIVEN AND TOSSED BY THE WIND."

EPHESIANS 4:27:

"AND DO NOT GIVE THE DEVIL AN OPPORTUNITY."

PROVERBS 21:23:

"HE WHO GUARDS HIS MOUTH AND HIS TONGUE, GUARDS HIS SOUL FROM TROUBLES."

JOHN 6:63:

"IT IS THE SPIRIT WHO GIVES LIFE; THE FLESH PROFITS NOTHING; THE WORDS THAT I HAVE SPOKEN TO YOU ARE SPIRIT AND ARE LIFE."

Confession:

Father God, I know Your Word contains spirit and life. I speak life into all my circumstances and I resurrect my Lazarus to come back to life. Be it dead end marriage, finances, career path, health. I confess that I am back to health and life. All conditions have turned around to my favor. New door of increase and multiplication has brought in long life of honor and love to win all situation to my favor. I am always in the face of God's abundance goodness and love. I declare that I am the only winner in this race before me and my enemies. Glory be to God for my life and more money and blesses flows in all directions to me.

"WE SOMETIMES HAVE TO SPEAK OUR MIND. BUT WE MUST USE WISDOM AND TACT AS WORDS CARRY POWER, HAVE LIFE, AND SPIRIT."

8

Worry-Free Life

....

To live your life free of worry is not always easy. Our eyes see our circumstances and our mind processes the image and the influence of the circumstance. Worrying will destroy you, and most of the time, you will miss the solution that is right by your face, since your focus is on worry and stress instead of on solution and an exit strategy. To live a life free from worry is to embrace the principle of surrendering everything to God who has the best method and strategy to bring solution to every need you may face.

Worry is a pain. It affects your immune system and spiritual atmosphere. It also breeds chaos in the life of your close friends and family. To live a worry-free life is to approach all circumstances with an open mind, trusting in God for a solution. Some situations are unavoidable, uncontrollable. However with calmness and with a cool head, you will dominate the environment, especially when we release everything into the care of God.

I now encourage you to meditate on these Bible verses:

COLOSSIANS 1:3:
"WE GIVE THANKS TO GOD, THE FATHER OF OUR LORD JESUS CHRIST, PRAYING ALWAYS FOR YOU."

ROMANS 8:2:
"FOR THE LAW OF THE SPIRIT OF LIFE IN CHRIST JESUS HAS SET YOU FREE FROM THE LAW OF SIN AND OF DEATH."

JOHN 14:1:
"DO NOT LET YOUR HEART BE TROUBLED; BELIEVE IN GOD, BELIEVE ALSO IN ME."

PHILIPPIANS 4:6:
"BE ANXIOUS FOR NOTHING, BUT IN EVERYTHING BY PRAYER AND SUPPLICATION WITH THANKSGIVING LET YOUR REQUESTS BE MADE KNOWN TO GOD."

PSALM 55:22:

"CAST YOUR BURDEN UPON THE LORD AND HE WILL SUSTAIN YOU; HE WILL NEVER ALLOW THE RIGHTEOUS TO BE SHAKEN."

HEBREWS 12:1-2:

"THEREFORE, SINCE WE HAVE SO GREAT A CLOUD OF WITNESSES SURROUNDING US, LET US ALSO LAY ASIDE EVERY ENCUMBRANCE AND THE SIN WHICH SO EASILY ENTANGLES US, AND LET US RUN WITH ENDURANCE THE RACE THAT IS SET BEFORE US, FIXING OUR EYES ON JESUS, THE AUTHOR AND PERFECTER OF FAITH, WHO FOR THE JOY SET BEFORE HIM ENDURED THE CROSS, DESPISING THE SHAME, AND HAS SAT DOWN AT THE RIGHT HAND OF THE THRONE OF GOD."

Confession:

I declare that from now, I will cast all my burdens onto Jesus and Him alone I will trust Him, to lead and guide me to arrive at my destination. Anything that troubles my mind, or worries my spirit, I surrender it in the hands of God. Jesus, you are my burden carrier and I take your blessings to be my inheritance from now. I live a life that is burden-free and worry-free, because Jesus carried my burden and I inherit His peace and joy in my life.

"TO LIVE A WORRY-FREE LIFE IS TO APPROACH ALL CIRCUMSTANCES WITH AN OPEN MIND, TRUSTING IN GOD FOR A SOLUTION."

9

Accept Jesus
As Your Savior

....

We all need a helping hand. There are some helping hands that are almost perfect, others are short-lived. Only Jesus' nail-pierced hands are perfect. Deciding to receive Jesus as your personal Savior and Lord brings you eternal security and contains all the ingredients for a life of peace and joy. One must decide where his salvation is coming from.

It is from this dimension that you will be able to get your blessings or suffer in this life. There is only one route to salvation and that is Jesus. All power and authority in Heaven, on earth and under the earth are contained in Jesus. Your salvation in Jesus is a passport to knowing the way forward in your life. Any other route will not and cannot lead you to salvation. It is short lived and not guaranteed to produce any lasting blessings.

I now encourage you to meditate on these Bible verses:

JOHN 3:16:
"FOR GOD SO LOVED THE WORLD THAT HE GAVE HIS ONLY BEGOTTEN SON, THAT WHOEVER BELIEVES IN HIM SHALL NOT PERISH, BUT HAVE ETERNAL LIFE."

JOHN 6:37:
"ALL THAT THE FATHER GIVES ME WILL COME TO ME, AND THE ONE WHO COMES TO ME I WILL CERTAINLY NOT CAST OUT."

JOHN 14:6:
"JESUS SAID TO HIM, I AM THE WAY, AND THE TRUTH, AND THE LIFE; NO ONE COMES TO THE FATHER BUT THROUGH ME."

JOHN 1:12:
"BUT AS MANY AS RECEIVED HIM, TO THEM HE GAVE

THE RIGHT TO BECOME CHILDREN OF GOD, EVEN
TO THOSE WHO BELIEVE IN HIS NAME."

EPHESIANS 2:1-10:
"AND YOU WERE DEAD IN YOUR TRESPASSES AND
SINS, IN WHICH YOU FORMERLY WALKED ACCORDING
TO THE COURSE OF THIS WORLD, ACCORDING TO
THE PRINCE OF THE POWER OF THE AIR, OF THE
SPIRIT THAT IS NOW WORKING IN THE SONS OF
DISOBEDIENCE. AMONG THEM WE TOO ALL FORMERLY
LIVED IN THE LUSTS OF OUR FLESH, INDULGING THE
DESIRES OF THE FLESH AND OF THE MIND, AND WERE
BY NATURE CHILDREN OF WRATH, EVEN AS THE REST.
BUT GOD, BEING RICH IN MERCY, BECAUSE OF HIS
GREAT LOVE WITH WHICH HE LOVED US, EVEN WHEN
WE WERE DEAD IN OUR TRANSGRESSIONS, MADE US
ALIVE TOGETHER WITH CHRIST (BY GRACE YOU HAVE
BEEN SAVED), AND RAISED US UP WITH HIM, AND
SEATED US WITH HIM IN THE HEAVENLY PLACES IN
CHRIST JESUS, SO THAT IN THE AGES TO COME HE
MIGHT SHOW THE SURPASSING RICHES OF HIS GRACE
IN KINDNESS TOWARD US IN CHRIST JESUS. FOR BY
GRACE YOU HAVE BEEN SAVED THROUGH FAITH; AND
THAT NOT OF YOURSELVES, IT IS THE GIFT OF GOD;
NOT AS A RESULT OF WORKS, SO THAT NO ONE MAY
BOAST. FOR WE ARE HIS WORKMANSHIP, CREATED
IN CHRIST JESUS FOR GOOD WORKS, WHICH GOD
PREPARED BEFOREHAND SO THAT WE WOULD WALK
IN THEM."

Confession:

I declare that hence from now on I surrender my old life

to the world, and embrace the new life of Jesus who is my Savior and Lord. Jesus come into my life and be my master. Have mercy on me. Forgive me of all my sins. Guide me in my new life as I submit my old life to Your Cross and under your precious blood. Let your light shine through me and remove all darkness away from me. I receive you Jesus as my personal Savior and Lord over my life, and I thank You for accepting me into your eternal Kingdom and glory. Let your peace rule in my world and my home.

10

Let The Holy Spirit Fill Your Life

....

A s a child of God, you owe it to yourself to reverence and breathe the Holy Spirit in every dimension of your life. The Holy Spirit is God sent to us by the Father and the Son. He is the master architect and the director of your life. Filling your life with the Holy Spirit can be compared to filling your car with gas. You will go a long way and you will arrive at your destination knowing full well that your light will not be dim. He is the energy and the source that empowers your success, and guarantees your deliverance from failure.

The Holy Spirit's in-filling will turn your life around as you hear His voice guiding you in the direction you must follow. To receive the in-filling of the Holy Spirit is absolutely necessary and every child of God must aim to achieve this blessed gift. All that you will ever need in this life is contained in the Holy Spirit.

I now encourage you to meditate on these Bible verses:

JOHN 14:16-17:
"I WILL ASK THE FATHER, AND HE WILL GIVE YOU ANOTHER HELPER, THAT HE MAY BE WITH YOU FOREVER; THAT IS THE SPIRIT OF TRUTH, WHOM THE WORLD CANNOT RECEIVE, BECAUSE IT DOES NOT SEE HIM OR KNOW HIM, BUT YOU KNOW HIM BECAUSE HE ABIDES WITH YOU AND WILL BE IN YOU."

ACTS 2:4:
"AND THEY WERE ALL FILLED WITH THE HOLY SPIRIT AND BEGAN TO SPEAK WITH OTHER TONGUES, AS THE SPIRIT WAS GIVING THEM UTTERANCE."

ACTS 8:12-17:
"BUT WHEN THEY BELIEVED PHILIP PREACHING THE GOOD NEWS ABOUT THE KINGDOM OF GOD

AND THE NAME OF JESUS CHRIST, THEY WERE BEING BAPTIZED, MEN AND WOMEN ALIKE. EVEN SIMON HIMSELF BELIEVED; AND AFTER BEING BAPTIZED, HE CONTINUED ON WITH PHILIP, AND AS HE OBSERVED SIGNS AND GREAT MIRACLES TAKING PLACE, HE WAS CONSTANTLY AMAZED. NOW WHEN THE APOSTLES IN JERUSALEM HEARD THAT SAMARIA HAD RECEIVED THE WORD OF GOD, THEY SENT THEM PETER AND JOHN, WHO CAME DOWN AND PRAYED FOR THEM THAT THEY MIGHT RECEIVE THE HOLY SPIRIT. FOR HE HAD NOT YET FALLEN UPON ANY OF THEM; THEY HAD SIMPLY BEEN BAPTIZED IN THE NAME OF THE LORD JESUS. THEN THEY BEGAN LAYING THEIR HANDS ON THEM, AND THEY WERE RECEIVING THE HOLY SPIRIT."

JUDE 1:20:
"BUT YOU, BELOVED, BUILDING YOURSELVES UP ON YOUR MOST HOLY FAITH, PRAYING IN THE HOLY SPIRIT."

ACTS 10:44-46:
"WHILE PETER WAS STILL SPEAKING THESE WORDS, THE HOLY SPIRIT FELL UPON ALL THOSE WHO WERE LISTENING TO THE MESSAGE. ALL THE CIRCUMCISED BELIEVERS WHO CAME WITH PETER WERE AMAZED, BECAUSE THE GIFT OF THE HOLY SPIRIT HAD BEEN POURED OUT ON THE GENTILES ALSO. FOR THEY WERE HEARING THEM SPEAKING WITH TONGUES AND EXALTING GOD. THEN PETER ANSWERED."

EPHESIANS 6:18:
"WITH ALL PRAYER AND PETITION PRAY AT ALL TIMES IN THE SPIRIT, AND WITH THIS IN VIEW, BE ON THE

ALERT WITH ALL PERSEVERANCE AND PETITION FOR ALL THE SAINTS."

Confession:

Holy Spirit I invite you into my life. Be my Lord and Principal. Fill my life with your presence, your voice and your power. I yield my life in your hands, that your voice will always speak and direct me to know which way I must go in the name of Jesus.

Holy Spirit be my consultant and my decision maker. I succumb my spirit, soul and body to you. I relent my thoughts and all that alarms me to you. Take over lord my life.

ISSUES
OF LIFE

II

Confidence

....

The Bible commands us to walk in boldness in all circumstances as Christ has overcome the world and the devil flees from us when we resist him. We owe it to ourselves to arrive at our destination successfully. Hence cowardice, timidity and fear cannot be allowed to cloud our judgement as we face life's challenging situations.

Jesus is as bold as a lion, and since he is our

mentor, we must pursue the route to conquer all, pursue all, and overtake all. Faith breeds boldness, as doubt creates fear. Walking in boldness changes the chemistry of success and elevates one's self to championship status. You can only succeed in life by walking in boldness, confidence, zeal and passion. Losers and cowardly people do not win in life. Not making your mind up to win eternally releases you into the island of failure and loneliness.

Be willing to embrace your destiny! Pay the price to have a life of joy, peace and fun! All it takes is confidence!

I now encourage you to meditate on these Bible verses:

PSALM 27:14:
"WAIT FOR THE LORD; BE STRONG AND LET YOUR HEART TAKE COURAGE; YES, WAIT FOR THE LORD."

HEBREWS 10:19:
"THEREFORE, BRETHREN, SINCE WE HAVE CONFIDENCE TO ENTER THE HOLY PLACE BY THE BLOOD OF JESUS."

ACTS 4:29:
"AND NOW, LORD, TAKE NOTE OF THEIR THREATS, AND GRANT THAT YOUR BOND-SERVANTS MAY SPEAK YOUR WORD WITH ALL CONFIDENCE."

HEBREWS 4:16:
"THEREFORE LET US DRAW NEAR WITH CONFIDENCE

TO THE THRONE OF GRACE, SO THAT WE MAY RECEIVE MERCY AND FIND GRACE TO HELP IN TIME OF NEED."

PROVERBS 28:1:
"THE WICKED FLEE WHEN NO ONE IS PURSUING, BUT THE RIGHTEOUS ARE BOLD AS A LION."

COLOSSIANS 2:10, 15:
"AND IN HIM YOU HAVE BEEN MADE COMPLETE, AND HE IS THE HEAD OVER ALL RULE AND AUTHORITY; WHEN HE HAD DISARMED THE RULERS AND AUTHORITIES, HE MADE A PUBLIC DISPLAY OF THEM, HAVING TRIUMPHED OVER THEM THROUGH HIM."

Confession:

Thank you Daddy God that my hope is built on you and my trust rests in you and upon you. I know you are with me and in all my circumstances and victory is always mine. I know I will not fail and no storm of life will overtake me because you are my confidence, protector and defender. Your mighty hand secures me to arrive at my purpose and my future is bright because greater is you who goes before me than all my other trusted friends. I am more than able to win and conquer all affairs of life through you oh lord of my life. You are mine sold rock upon which I stand on.

"JESUS IS AS BOLD AS A LION, AND SINCE HE IS OUR MENTOR, WE MUST PURSUE THE ROUTE TO CONQUER ALL, PURSUE ALL, AND OVERTAKE ALL."

12

Husbands

....

The husband is the head of the family as Christ is the Head of His church, and Head of the family. One must pay attention to the Godly wisdom and leadership of Christ in their life as they lead their family. Leadership is not always strength, but wisdom, knowledge and wise counsel.

As husband, you must walk in boldness, integrity and character that inspire and challenge others to aspire towards Christ leadership style. God requires you as a husband to lead a wholesome life that brings blessings and confidence to your family and God's kingdom. As king and priest of your household, you must be filled with the wisdom of God and with knowledge and understanding of His word to be able to rule your life and your household.

I now encourage you to meditate on these Bible verses:

PROVERBS 3:3:
"DO NOT LET KINDNESS AND TRUTH LEAVE YOU; BIND THEM AROUND YOUR NECK, WRITE THEM ON THE TABLET OF YOUR HEART."

PROVERBS 2:2:
"MAKE YOUR EAR ATTENTIVE TO WISDOM, INCLINE YOUR HEART TO UNDERSTANDING."

PROVERBS 6:22:
"WHEN YOU WALK ABOUT, THEY WILL GUIDE YOU; WHEN YOU SLEEP, THEY WILL WATCH OVER YOU; AND WHEN YOU AWAKE, THEY WILL TALK TO YOU."

PROVERBS 1:33:
"BUT HE WHO LISTENS TO ME SHALL LIVE SECURELY. AND WILL BE AT EASE FROM THE DREAD OF EVIL."

1 PETER 3:7-9:
"YOU HUSBANDS IN THE SAME WAY, LIVE WITH YOUR WIVES IN AN UNDERSTANDING WAY, AS WITH

SOMEONE WEAKER, SINCE SHE IS A WOMAN; AND SHOW HER HONOR AS A FELLOW HEIR OF THE GRACE OF LIFE, SO THAT YOUR PRAYERS WILL NOT BE HINDERED. TO SUM UP, ALL OF YOU BE HARMONIOUS, SYMPATHETIC, BROTHERLY, KIND HEARTED, AND HUMBLE IN SPIRIT; NOT RETURNING EVIL FOR EVIL OR INSULT FOR INSULT, BUT GIVING A BLESSING INSTEAD; FOR YOU WERE CALLED FOR THE VERY PURPOSE THAT YOU MIGHT INHERIT A BLESSING."

PROVERBS 11:30:
"THE FRUIT OF THE RIGHTEOUS IS A TREE OF LIFE, AND HE WHO IS WISE WINS SOULS."

Confession:

Father God, as I walk in the capacity as a husband in my family, I ask you for your divine insight to know how to be a faithful shepherd and a foundation builder in my marriage. Let your grace and mercy direct me and lead me to stand in the gap for my family. As Jesus became my sacrifice, lead me to be a faithful servant to serve my family. I thank you for honoring me as the head of the family. I receive your wisdom and guidance to lead my household. I know that you have blessed me with all that is necessary to take my family to the next level. I glorify your name for my family.

"ONE MUST PAY ATTENTION TO THE GODLY WISDOM AND LEADERSHIP OF CHRIST IN THEIR LIFE AS THEY LEAD THEIR FAMILY."

13

Wives

....

As a woman of God your character, temperament and mood will bring blessings to your family. As you walk in this capacity, your lamp must shine and burn throughout all troubles, and all circumstances of life. You can be a door opener, and a channel of blessings to your family in spirit, soul and body. Your strength and your dignity become your clothing which shepherds and influences all those that come into your sphere. As you open your mouth, you must carry blessings, happiness and praise.

You must release healing, love and care which create an atmosphere for success and excellence. Comfort your children in their time of need. Be a helpmate to your husband. As a wife, avoid idleness, gossip, self-pity and devious behavior that divide your family and create chaos around your loved ones.

A beautiful woman does not come with makeup, but from within. Aspire to beautiful from the inside out, and your external environment will correspond to your beauty. You can always buy make at any day or at anytime. The day you have no makeup on, you will look ugly. Flow from within and you will be beautiful.

I now encourage you to meditate on these Bible verses:

PROVERBS 31:10-31:
"AN EXCELLENT WIFE, WHO CAN FIND? FOR HER WORTH IS FAR ABOVE JEWELS. THE HEART OF HER HUSBAND TRUSTS IN HER, AND HE WILL HAVE NO LACK OF GAIN. SHE DOES HIM GOOD AND NOT EVIL ALL THE DAYS OF HER LIFE. SHE LOOKS FOR WOOL AND FLAX AND WORKS WITH HER HANDS IN DELIGHT. SHE IS LIKE MERCHANT SHIPS; SHE BRINGS HER FOOD FROM AFAR. SHE RISES ALSO WHILE IT IS STILL NIGHT AND GIVES FOOD TO HER HOUSEHOLD AND PORTIONS TO HER MAIDENS. SHE CONSIDERS A FIELD AND BUYS IT; FROM HER EARNINGS SHE PLANTS

A VINEYARD. SHE GIRDS HERSELF WITH STRENGTH AND MAKES HER ARMS STRONG. SHE SENSES THAT HER GAIN IS GOOD; HER LAMP DOES NOT GO OUT AT NIGHT. SHE STRETCHES OUT HER HANDS TO THE DISTAFF, AND HER HANDS GRASP THE SPINDLE. SHE EXTENDS HER HAND TO THE POOR, AND SHE STRETCHES OUT HER HANDS TO THE NEEDY. SHE IS NOT AFRAID OF THE SNOW FOR HER HOUSEHOLD, FOR ALL HER HOUSEHOLD ARE CLOTHED WITH SCARLET. SHE MAKES COVERINGS FOR HERSELF; HER CLOTHING IS FINE LINEN AND PURPLE. HER HUSBAND IS KNOWN IN THE GATES, WHEN HE SITS AMONG THE ELDERS OF THE LAND. SHE MAKES LINEN GARMENTS AND SELLS THEM, AND SUPPLIES BELTS TO THE TRADESMEN. STRENGTH AND DIGNITY ARE HER CLOTHING, AND SHE SMILES AT THE FUTURE. SHE OPENS HER MOUTH IN WISDOM, AND THE TEACHING OF KINDNESS IS ON HER TONGUE. SHE LOOKS WELL TO THE WAYS OF HER HOUSEHOLD, AND DOES NOT EAT THE BREAD OF IDLENESS. HER CHILDREN RISE UP AND BLESS HER; HER HUSBAND ALSO, AND HE PRAISES HER, SAYING: MANY DAUGHTERS HAVE DONE NOBLY, BUT YOU EXCEL THEM ALL. CHARM IS DECEITFUL AND BEAUTY IS VAIN, BUT A WOMAN WHO FEARS THE LORD, SHE SHALL BE PRAISED. GIVE HER THE PRODUCT OF HER HANDS, AND LET HER WORKS PRAISE HER IN THE GATES."

Confessions:

As your chosen handmaid, I thank you for causing me to march in wisdom and knowledge as I walk and help build my family. I trust your presence to make me a wise daughter of Zion to be there as a help mate with my husband to build our household. May your name be praised and glorified as I walk in my capacity as a wife. I thank you for giving me understanding, awareness and grace to love my husband and my children.

Thank you for causing me to work and cooperate with my household to build a home of peace and love for all. I glorify you oh Lord for your continuous blessing and favor for my home. I thank you for my dear husband and kids who are the next generation.

"YOU MUST RELEASE HEALING, LOVE AND CARE WHICH CREATE AN ATMOSPHERE FOR SUCCESS AND EXCELLENCE."

14

Peaceful Marriage

....

All marriages can only succeed where love, unity and understanding prevail. Your decision to be part of a marriage circle requires your personal contribution and conviction of your path in the security of the union. Harmony only comes when two people agree to walk together. A marriage built on unity and love will always create an atmosphere of blessings, an atmosphere of fruitfulness and an atmosphere of multiplication. Harmonious marriages breed an untold and unlimited number of blessings which affect generations now and generations after.

They also create a legacy for future generations. A marriage united in strength creates increase and multiplication of God`s eternal blessings on our offspring. One must walk in unity to breed success, stability and growth.

I now encourage you to meditate on these Bible verses:

ROMANS 5:5:
"AND HOPE DOES NOT DISAPPOINT, BECAUSE THE LOVE OF GOD HAS BEEN POURED OUT WITHIN OUR HEARTS THROUGH THE HOLY SPIRIT WHO WAS GIVEN TO US."

PHILIPPIANS 1:9:
"AND THIS I PRAY, THAT YOUR LOVE MAY ABOUND STILL MORE AND MORE IN REAL KNOWLEDGE AND ALL DISCERNMENT."

EPHESIANS 4:32:
"BE KIND TO ONE ANOTHER, TENDER-HEARTED, FORGIVING EACH OTHER, JUST AS GOD IN CHRIST ALSO HAS FORGIVEN YOU."

JEREMIAH 1:12:
"THEN THE LORD SAID TO ME, YOU HAVE SEEN WELL, FOR I AM WATCHING OVER MY WORD TO PERFORM IT."

1 PETER 3:7:
"YOU HUSBANDS IN THE SAME WAY, LIVE WITH YOUR WIVES IN AN UNDERSTANDING WAY, AS WITH SOMEONE WEAKER, SINCE SHE IS A WOMAN; AND SHOW HER HONOR AS A FELLOW HEIR OF THE GRACE OF LIFE, SO THAT YOUR PRAYERS WILL NOT BE HINDERED."

ISAIAH 32:17
"AND THE WORK OF RIGHTEOUSNESS WILL BE PEACE, AND THE SERVICE OF RIGHTEOUSNESS, QUIETNESS AND CONFIDENCE FOREVER."

Confession:

Father God, make me a frequency of your peace and cause me to walk seeking peace at all times. I thank you for making me a harmony lover and a peace seeker. I glorify you that through your peace over my life, I will radiate the affection and peace of Christ in every circumstance everywhere that I go. May your name be praised as I become an example of Christ's peace to lift up those who are caught up in the war of chaos and confusion in their life. Let your peace lead me to be a system of reconciliation to others, and a river of joy for love ones to swim in and arrive at their destination. Let me decree in peace and bring others into your stream of harmony and pleasure. Let my life be an instrument of your grace and honor to polish each event to radiate your overcoming peace.

"HARMONIOUS MARRIAGES BREED AN UNTOLD AND UNLIMITED NUMBER OF BLESSINGS WHICH AFFECT GENERATIONS NOW AND GENERATIONS AFTER."

15

Cordiality In Marriage

....

Two people can only walk together when they are united in purpose, by the love of God, and are compatible in chemistry, character and conscience. Darkness and light cannot walk side by side in any marriage. Like-minded people will have greater strength to achieve greater strength and abundance. Synergy in marriage will always produce a beautiful and a wonderful peace and joy in each other's lives. Moving in this atmosphere makes the storms of life easy and faster to conquer. It secures families, breeds success and multiplication in the work of one's hands. It makes the journey of life much easier and accommodating, thereby creating fruitfulness and a quick turnaround in every negative circumstance with the battles of life becoming easier to conquer. Two people can only walk together when they are compatible, in agreement and united in their vision, aspirations and goals.

I now encourage you to meditate on these Bible verses:

1 CORINTHIANS 13:4-8:
"LOVE IS PATIENT, LOVE IS KIND AND IS NOT JEALOUS; LOVE DOES NOT BRAG AND IS NOT ARROGANT, DOES NOT ACT UNBECOMINGLY; IT DOES NOT SEEK ITS OWN, IS NOT PROVOKED, DOES NOT TAKE INTO ACCOUNT A WRONG SUFFERED, DOES NOT REJOICE IN UNRIGHTEOUSNESS, BUT REJOICES WITH THE TRUTH; BEARS ALL THINGS, BELIEVES ALL THINGS, HOPES ALL THINGS, ENDURES ALL THINGS. LOVE NEVER FAILS; BUT IF THERE ARE GIFTS OF PROPHECY, THEY WILL BE DONE AWAY; IF THERE ARE TONGUES, THEY WILL CEASE; IF THERE IS KNOWLEDGE, IT WILL BE DONE AWAY."

1 CORINTHIANS 14:1:

"PURSUE LOVE, YET DESIRE EARNESTLY SPIRITUAL GIFTS, BUT ESPECIALLY THAT YOU MAY PROPHESY."

EPHESIANS 5:1-2:

"THEREFORE BE IMITATORS OF GOD, AS BELOVED CHILDREN; AND WALK IN LOVE, JUST AS CHRIST ALSO LOVED YOU AND GAVE HIMSELF UP FOR US, AN OFFERING AND A SACRIFICE TO GOD AS A FRAGRANT AROMA."

Confession:

Holy Spirit, let me to be a unity designer and a harmony pursuer so that my home and I will inherit your blessings and your favor. I thank you for blessing my marriage. Your Holy Spirit holds us together as one united family. Glory be to your name that my house and I will always serve together, win together knowing that you are at the helm of our family. May Your Holy Spirit continuously shadow my home and me to love, serve and honor you. Thank you for blessing my marriage moving us into the overflow of your goodness.

"SYNERGY IN MARRIAGE WILL ALWAYS PRODUCE A BEAUTIFUL AND A WONDERFUL PEACE AND JOY IN EACH OTHER'S LIVES. MOVING IN THIS ATMOSPHERE MAKES THE STORMS OF LIFE EASY AND FASTER TO CONQUER. IT SECURES FAMILIES, BREEDS SUCCESS AND MULTIPLICATION IN THE WORK OF ONE'S HANDS."

16
Children Of Inheritance

....

Children are the end result of a union of two: father and mother. Children are a blessing and are generational carriers. Therefore their welfare and wellbeing are supreme and vital. They are to be supported and guided in all circumstances of life.

They are invaluable assets worth protecting and securing. Nothing must be allowed to impede this function. Their presence creates joy, peace and stirs up an atmosphere of noise, delight and fun.

Having children is a thoughtful and a challenging quest. Their creation overrides pain and chaos when we give our all to sustain and maintain their life. As they grow, they become the fruits in our garden. Their fruits become tasty depending on how we originally planted them. They sometimes provoke and irritate, but they are an asset which is priceless and invaluable to supersede the initial investment.

I now encourage you to meditate on these Bible verses:

JEREMIAH 1:12:
"THEN THE LORD SAID TO ME, YOU HAVE SEEN WELL, FOR I AM WATCHING OVER MY WORD TO PERFORM IT."

ISAIAH 54:13:
"ALL YOUR SONS WILL BE TAUGHT OF THE LORD; AND THE WELLBEING OF YOUR SONS WILL BE GREAT."

1 PETER 5:7:
"CASTING ALL YOUR ANXIETY ON HIM, BECAUSE HE CARES FOR YOU."

PROVERBS 22:6:
"TRAIN UP A CHILD IN THE WAY HE SHOULD GO, EVEN WHEN HE IS OLD HE WILL NOT DEPART FROM IT."

PSALM 8:1-2:

"O LORD, OUR LORD, HOW MAJESTIC IS YOUR NAME IN ALL THE EARTH, WHO HAVE DISPLAYED YOUR SPLENDOR ABOVE THE HEAVENS! FROM THE MOUTH OF INFANTS AND NURSING BABES YOU HAVE ESTABLISHED STRENGTH BECAUSE OF YOUR ADVERSARIES, TO MAKE THE ENEMY AND THE REVENGEFUL CEASE."

PSALM 9:2-3:

"I WILL BE GLAD AND EXULT IN YOU; I WILL SING PRAISE TO YOUR NAME, O MOST HIGH. WHEN MY ENEMIES TURN BACK, THEY STUMBLE AND PERISH BEFORE YOU."

Confession:

Glorious one, thank you for blessing and making me a fruitful vine. Thank you for giving me children of honor and of grace. I know that my children are blessed and they are the successful vine coming out of your goodness and your mercy. I declare that my children shall inherit and possess the birthright of Christ Jesus to walk in obedience and love. My children are productive vines and wherever they go, they are a blessing to their peers and a fragrance of joy to their environment. I surrender my children into your mighty hands and I trust that my born children and adopted children will always rest Under Your watchful eyes. Thank You for honoring my children with life and blessings. I love you for defending my generation and my dynasty.

"CHILDREN ARE A BLESSING AND ARE GENERATIONAL CARRIERS."

17

My Family Home

....

A home is a shelter that must be covered
and protected at all costs. A leaky home
and a miserable, sad home will always
produce negative energy which in the
end will destroy the contents. A home built
on the foundation of Christ Jesus will result
in an atmosphere of celebration. As Christ
becomes the center of the home, so also His
blessings become the end result of the family.
When God is taken out of the home,

self and Satan take over. Troubles and inconsistencies become the order of the day. Allowing God to be the head of the home stabilizes the family and steers ahead the boat of life to arrive successfully at her destination. A home without God is like a soccer field without order. Any home that refuses God's presence and order exposes the home to the destructive elements of life and society. Any home that allows God to be the author and the finisher will always successfully arrive at their destination.

I now encourage you to meditate on these Bible verses:

EPHESIANS 1:3:
"BLESSED BE THE GOD AND FATHER OF OUR LORD JESUS CHRIST, WHO HAS BLESSED US WITH EVERY SPIRITUAL BLESSING IN THE HEAVENLY PLACES IN CHRIST."

ACTS 16:31:
"THEY SAID, BELIEVE IN THE LORD JESUS, AND YOU WILL BE SAVED, YOU AND YOUR HOUSEHOLD."

PHILIPPIANS 2:10-11:
"SO THAT AT THE NAME OF JESUS EVERY KNEE WILL BOW, OF THOSE WHO ARE IN HEAVEN AND ON EARTH AND UNDER THE EARTH, AND THAT EVERY TONGUE WILL CONFESS THAT JESUS CHRIST IS LORD, TO THE GLORY OF GOD THE FATHER."

ACTS 20:32:
"AND NOW I COMMEND YOU TO GOD AND TO THE WORD OF HIS GRACE, WHICH IS ABLE TO BUILD YOU UP AND TO GIVE YOU THE INHERITANCE AMONG ALL THOSE WHO ARE SANCTIFIED."

COLOSSIANS 3:23:
"WHATEVER YOU DO, DO YOUR WORK HEARTILY, AS FOR THE LORD RATHER THAN FOR MEN."

COLOSSIANS 3:14-15:
"BEYOND ALL THESE THINGS PUT ON LOVE, WHICH IS THE PERFECT BOND OF UNITY. LET THE PEACE OF CHRIST RULE IN YOUR HEARTS, TO WHICH INDEED YOU WERE CALLED IN ONE BODY; AND BE THANKFUL."

Confession:

Sweet Jesus I glorify and thank you that your grace and mercy form the roof over my family. I honor you for being the night shadow and the day cloud which lead and protect my family home. For all I possess in my family, I recognize you. I thank you that they break under your goodness and your mercy. I know that my family household rests under your massive defense and love. My domestic home-based is under Your Holy Spirit and Your Holy angels are always on assignment to continually protect my intimate home. I release your sanctified blood to surround my property, the front and the back of my house that no open entrance becomes the enemy's foothold. For Your mighty protection secures me and my family home.

"ANY HOME THAT ALLOWS
GOD TO BE THE AUTHOR AND
THE FINISHER WILL ALWAYS
SUCCESSFULLY ARRIVE AT THEIR
DESTINATION."

18

Prosperity
& Success

....

God desires that all His creation experiences prosperity of life, soul and body. Walking in prosperity is a journey and a process that require an intimate attention to instructions and details. Prosperity is an end journey and cannot be attained casually without discipline and diligence. Hard work based on the wisdom of God and the understanding of God's principles always guarantees success and peace.

Lack of knowledge of the Word of God and His way of doing things always creates disorder and mistakes. One may strive to gather all and possess all, but at the end will lose it if God is not the center of the gathering. Prosperity as a whole is great and must be desired and sought to be achieved. But it must be done with God as the center of it all.

I now encourage you to meditate on these Bible verses:

ISAIAH 55:11:
"SO WILL MY WORD BE WHICH GOES FORTH FROM MY MOUTH; IT WILL NOT RETURN TO ME EMPTY, WITHOUT ACCOMPLISHING WHAT I DESIRE, AND WITHOUT SUCCEEDING IN THE MATTER FOR WHICH I SENT IT."

PHILIPPIANS 4:9:
"THE THINGS YOU HAVE LEARNED AND RECEIVED AND HEARD AND SEEN IN ME, PRACTICE THESE THINGS, AND THE GOD OF PEACE WILL BE WITH YOU."

COLOSSIANS 1:13:
"FOR HE RESCUED US FROM THE DOMAIN OF DARKNESS, AND TRANSFERRED US TO THE KINGDOM OF HIS BELOVED SON."

PSALM 46:1:

"GOD IS OUR REFUGE AND STRENGTH, A VERY PRESENT HELP IN TROUBLE."

MATTHEW 18:18:

"TRULY I SAY TO YOU, WHATEVER YOU BIND ON EARTH SHALL HAVE BEEN BOUND IN HEAVEN; AND WHATEVER YOU LOOSE ON EARTH SHALL HAVE BEEN LOOSED IN HEAVEN."

PHILIPPIANS 4:19:

"AND MY GOD WILL SUPPLY ALL YOUR NEEDS ACCORDING TO HIS RICHES IN GLORY IN CHRIST JESUS."

Confession:

It is your will and desire that I walk in prosperity and health even as my soul prospers. I thank you that you have chosen me to be an inheritor of your blessings. As Your word releases blessings upon me, may your divine revelation and insight into your expression become my passion? I know you have blessed me as I minister always in your word. Your word of life will lead me onto a fruitful and a successful journey. I thank you that your word of life has caused me to be an asset to mankind. Let your blessings and your good success continuously reign over my life that wherever I go, I will exhibit Christ's favor and anointing to attract more blessings. Thank you for giving me insight to know how to generate activities that promote prosperity and success in my life.

"HARD WORK BASED ON THE WISDOM OF GOD AND THE UNDERSTANDING OF GOD'S PRINCIPLES ALWAYS GUARANTEES SUCCESS AND PEACE."

19

Honoring God With Your Finances

....

Confessing over your tithes is an instrument of attracting God's eternal blessings on the work of your hands. Dedicating your tithes to God draws his blessings and His grace in opening the avenue of life to succeed. Even though it is a command, it is an honor to carry out the obedience of tithing. Giving and receiving is part of life. Tithing is one channel of giving while honoring God is a channel of receiving.

As we put God first in our tithing, God releases His eternal blessings on us and our family. He stops the devourer from tampering with our blessings and our tithe becomes a spiritual life insurance for our whole family.

Be a financial champion! Take your dominion over money!

I now encourage you to meditate on these Bible verses:

COLOSSIANS 1:13:
"FOR HE RESCUED US FROM THE DOMAIN OF DARKNESS, AND TRANSFERRED US TO THE KINGDOM OF HIS BELOVED SON."

EPHESIANS 2:1-5:
"AND YOU WERE DEAD IN YOUR TRESPASSES AND SINS, IN WHICH YOU FORMERLY WALKED ACCORDING TO THE COURSE OF THIS WORLD, ACCORDING TO THE PRINCE OF THE POWER OF THE AIR, OF THE SPIRIT THAT IS NOW WORKING IN THE SONS OF DISOBEDIENCE. AMONG THEM WE TOO ALL FORMERLY LIVED IN THE LUSTS OF OUR FLESH, INDULGING THE DESIRES OF THE FLESH AND OF THE MIND, AND WERE BY NATURE CHILDREN OF WRATH, EVEN AS THE REST. BUT GOD, BEING RICH IN MERCY, BECAUSE OF HIS GREAT LOVE WITH WHICH HE LOVED US, EVEN WHEN WE WERE DEAD IN OUR TRANSGRESSIONS, MADE US

ALIVE TOGETHER WITH CHRIST (BY GRACE YOU HAVE BEEN SAVED)."

HEBREWS 3:1:
"THEREFORE, HOLY BRETHREN, PARTAKERS OF A HEAVENLY CALLING, CONSIDER JESUS, THE APOSTLE AND HIGH PRIEST OF OUR CONFESSION."

Confession:

Father God, all that I possess and all that I have has come from you. Since you are the source of all creation, I glorify you with the fruit of my hands. Silver and gold are yours and I acknowledge that truth. Receive all that my hands have produced as my offering and sacrifice of praise. I will give you first place in all my finances and will honor you with the fruit of my labor. Let your glorious blessings be upon the work of my hands that I will experience your multiplication blessings and be a blessing to the Kingdom of God. Create in me a mindset to be a Kingdom promoter and impart in me the passion to be a Kingdom sponsor. I thank you that I am a blessing and a joy to the household of faith.

"DEDICATING YOUR TITHES TO GOD ATTRACTS HIS BLESSINGS AND HIS GRACE IN OPENING THE AVENUE OF LIFE TO SUCCEED."

20

Walking In Health

....

It is the will of God that we should walk and be in health in all areas of our life. Our path is to appropriate the Word of God which is Jesus Incarnate in His Word to affect all zones of our life. Health and healing can only come to us if we abide within God's order of love. Strength and healing are necessary if we are to succeed and maintain a happy life. Walking in fitness opens many avenues to enjoy the fruitfulness of this earth, and to run the race of contentment with our family and friends. God desires that we walk in power and we must unite with Him to enjoy this blessing which converts into prosperity in all our activities of life.

Health and healing become the cornerstone of our life and we must cherish every circumstance to uphold this quest. God desires that you live long and be in vigor even as our soul prospers, but we must always position ourselves to take advantage of this promise. Without health, life is miserable and we are at the mercy of others and medications. Aspire to be strong and God's eternal blessings will reign upon you.

I now encourage you to meditate on these Bible verses:

PSALM 91:1:
"HE WHO DWELLS IN THE SHELTER OF THE MOST HIGH WILL ABIDE IN THE SHADOW OF THE ALMIGHTY."

PSALM 112:7:
"HE WILL NOT FEAR EVIL TIDINGS; HIS HEART IS STEADFAST, TRUSTING IN THE LORD."

EPHESIANS 6:11, 16:
"PUT ON THE FULL ARMOR OF GOD, SO THAT YOU WILL BE ABLE TO STAND FIRM AGAINST THE SCHEMES OF THE DEVIL. IN ADDITION TO ALL, TAKING UP THE SHIELD OF FAITH WITH WHICH YOU WILL BE ABLE TO EXTINGUISH ALL THE FLAMING ARROWS OF THE EVIL ONE."

HEBREWS 4:12:

"FOR THE WORD OF GOD IS LIVING AND ACTIVE
AND SHARPER THAN ANY TWO-EDGED SWORD, AND
PIERCING AS FAR AS THE DIVISION OF SOUL AND SPIRIT,
OF BOTH JOINTS AND MARROW, AND ABLE TO JUDGE
THE THOUGHTS AND INTENTIONS OF THE HEART."

PSALM 91:10:

"NO EVIL WILL BEFALL YOU, NOR WILL ANY PLAGUE
COME NEAR YOUR TENT."

PSALM 34:7:

"THE ANGEL OF THE LORD ENCAMPS AROUND THOSE
WHO FEAR HIM, AND RESCUES THEM."

Confession:

*I walk in health and wholeness in my spirit, soul and
body. No sickness of any kind known to man, physically
and spiritually has control over my life and that of my
household. I rest under your mighty hand of protection and
love. Therefore, no disease of the kingdom of darkness will
prevail against my spirit, soul and body. I am healed and
I walk in total health by the refinement of God's blessings.
I am an energetic vine and I draw the fresh grace and
oil of gladness to wash and surround my spirit, soul and
body. The blood of Jesus preserves me to tread in complete
harmony. No ailment has any hold upon my life. I reject
every infliction and complaint of curses from the spirit of
darkness over my life. I am a fruitful and a strong vine*

drawing life and power from Jesus my Savior, I am part of the True Vine.

"THE BLOOD OF JESUS PRESERVES ME IN ALL CIRCUMSTANCES OF MY LIFE."

21

Security

....

Walking in safety requires us to have a relationship with our guardian angel through the instructions of the Almighty God. Life is too complicated to walk in sloppiness and disorder. Disobeying the laws of safety and order will destroy and cut short every pleasure that one desires to attain in life. Your safety in life requires your participation and contribution. We are always responsible for all the outcomes of our life. It is totally impossible to be happy where we dishonor the laws of safety and security.

Doing things foolishly and expecting a positive outcome is tantamount to wickedness and negligence for your own life. There is only one life and you must uphold it with all responsibility, care and honor. If you lose your safety net you will be hurt. So be wise and careful in preserving your safety net. God desires that you walk in law and order which creates a protection net for happiness in this life.

I now encourage you to meditate on these Bible verses:

JEREMIAH 1:12:
"THEN THE LORD SAID TO ME, YOU HAVE SEEN WELL, FOR I AM WATCHING OVER MY WORD TO PERFORM IT."

PSALM 91:10:
"NO EVIL WILL BEFALL YOU, NOR WILL ANY PLAGUE COME NEAR YOUR TENT."

PSALM 3:5:
"I LAY DOWN AND SLEPT; I AWOKE, FOR THE LORD SUSTAINS ME."

PSALM 4:8:
"IN PEACE I WILL BOTH LIE DOWN AND SLEEP, FOR YOU ALONE, O LORD, MAKE ME TO DWELL IN SAFETY."

ISAIAH 26:3:
"THE STEADFAST OF MIND YOU WILL KEEP IN PERFECT PEACE, BECAUSE HE TRUSTS IN YOU."

PROVERBS 3:24:
"WHEN YOU LIE DOWN, YOU WILL NOT BE AFRAID; WHEN YOU LIE DOWN, YOUR SLEEP WILL BE SWEET."

Confession:

I glorify your holy name for I rest under the shadow of You, Almighty God. I thank you that your holy angels on assignment are protecting me and securing my life through the passage of this present world's system. I know I am secured and safe under your mighty hand. Your glorious protection by cloud by day and your fire by night secures my safekeeping and wellbeing in this life.

I thank you Father God that I am safe and locked under your watchful eyes and your mighty hands surround my habitation. I will rest in the shadow of your glory and peace. Thank you Lord that I am sheltered and my welfare and good are secured.

"DOING THINGS FOOLISHLY AND EXPECTING A POSITIVE OUTCOME IS TANTAMOUNT TO WICKEDNESS AND NEGLIGENCE FOR YOUR OWN LIFE. THERE IS ONLY ONE LIFE AND YOU MUST UPHOLD IT WITH ALL RESPONSIBILITY, CARE AND HONOR."

22

Conquering Fear

You can have victory if you choose to walk in boldness and select to win without concealing and entertaining any cowardice or fear. It is the desire of God that you walk in victory in all circumstances of life. Given that life has many faces it is very important that one's mind is made up to achieve victory without compromising hard work, talent, knowledge and ability. God rewards good stewardship and boldness to create victory. Fear is a product of doubt as victory is a product of faith and bravery. One must choose victory over fear. Fear destroys, delays and hurts.

It imprisons thoughts, ideas and happiness. Victory is an instrument of celebration and everyone loves victory over fear. Ignoring fear enables you to focus on achieving your goal. Though there are challenges in life and sometimes situations are too complicated to understand, your mind is the key to determine the direction and timing for God to release His blessings on one's effort. Victory will be secured when we release fear and doubt, and proceed in faith.

I now encourage you to meditate on these Bible verses:

ISAIAH 54:17:
"NO WEAPON THAT IS FORMED AGAINST YOU WILL PROSPER; AND EVERY TONGUE THAT ACCUSES YOU IN JUDGMENT YOU WILL CONDEMN. THIS IS THE HERITAGE OF THE SERVANTS OF THE LORD, AND THEIR VINDICATION IS FROM ME, DECLARES THE LORD."

PSALM 91:1:
"HE WHO DWELLS IN THE SHELTER OF THE MOST HIGH WILL ABIDE IN THE SHADOW OF THE ALMIGHTY."

PROVERBS 3:6, 8:
"IN ALL YOUR WAYS ACKNOWLEDGE HIM, AND HE WILL MAKE YOUR PATHS STRAIGHT. IT WILL BE HEALING TO YOUR BODY AND REFRESHMENT TO YOUR BONES."

PSALM 138:8:

"THE LORD WILL ACCOMPLISH WHAT CONCERNS ME; YOUR LOVINGKINDNESS, O LORD, IS EVERLASTING; DO NOT FORSAKE THE WORKS OF YOUR HANDS."

EPHESIANS 3:16:

"THAT HE WOULD GRANT YOU, ACCORDING TO THE RICHES OF HIS GLORY, TO BE STRENGTHENED WITH POWER THROUGH HIS SPIRIT IN THE INNER MAN."

ISAIAH 49:25:

"SURELY, THUS SAYS THE LORD, EVEN THE CAPTIVES OF THE MIGHTY MAN WILL BE TAKEN AWAY, AND THE PREY OF THE TYRANT WILL BE RESCUED; FOR I WILL CONTEND WITH THE ONE WHO CONTENDS WITH YOU, AND I WILL SAVE YOUR SONS."

Confession:

I glorify your name and I declare that no weapon formed against me shall prosper. I know that you and I are walking in total victory and we are the majority in all circumstances of life.

No weapon of darkness or arrows of the noon day or shadows of the early hour of the morning from Satan will prevail against me. No principalities and powers or spiritual wickedness in high places on assignment will prevail against me.

In the name of Jesus, I am shielded and protected from all visible and invisible forces. I conquer every known and unknown force against my destiny. I declare that no fear spirit of any kind, shape or form will preside and prevail against my destiny.

I am chosen to be a winner and a conqueror because Jesus is the head and master of my life. Heaven and earth backs me up. Because greater is He (Jesus) who is in me than all.

23
Conquering Depression

....

Depression is a situation where one's mind and environment are overshadowed by darkness. Happiness no longer resides in the person. It causes feelings of sadness and or a loss of interest in activities once enjoyed. One may need intensive prayer, love and care to overcome gloom. Overcoming depression is a spiritual problem, not a physical problem. As you seek God through fasting and Holy Spirit inspired prayers, the evil spirit is conquered and the individual deliverance is released. That wicked spirit will is broken. It may require that your family members fast for you if you are not able to. Finally, divine intervention must be employed to overcome that spiritual burden.

Having done it all, bring yourself under the leadership of the Holy Spirit so that any ancestral curses or access points in one's life will be destroyed. Praying and fasting are the keys to breaking the spirit of depression, irrespective of any physical medication. Anyone suffering from depression can come out clean and clear. It requires the approach of the God-centered deliverance system.

I now encourage you to meditate on these Bible verses:

PSALM 9:10:
"AND THOSE WHO KNOW YOUR NAME WILL PUT THEIR TRUST IN YOU, FOR YOU, O LORD, HAVE NOT FORSAKEN THOSE WHO SEEK YOU."

EPHESIANS 4:27:
"AND DO NOT GIVE THE DEVIL AN OPPORTUNITY."

HEBREWS 12:12-13:
"THEREFORE, STRENGTHEN THE HANDS THAT ARE WEAK AND THE KNEES THAT ARE FEEBLE, AND MAKE

STRAIGHT PATHS FOR YOUR FEET, SO THAT THE LIMB WHICH IS LAME MAY NOT BE PUT OUT OF JOINT, BUT RATHER BE HEALED."

GALATIANS 1:4:
"WHO GAVE HIMSELF FOR OUR SINS SO THAT HE MIGHT RESCUE US FROM THIS PRESENT EVIL AGE, ACCORDING TO THE WILL OF OUR GOD AND FATHER,"

NEHEMIAH 8:10:
THEN HE SAID TO THEM, "GO, EAT OF THE FAT, DRINK OF THE SWEET, AND SEND PORTIONS TO HIM WHO HAS NOTHING PREPARED; FOR THIS DAY IS HOLY TO OUR LORD. DO NOT BE GRIEVED, FOR THE JOY OF THE LORD IS YOUR STRENGTH."

JOHN 14:27:
"PEACE I LEAVE WITH YOU; MY PEACE I GIVE TO YOU; NOT AS THE WORLD GIVES DO I GIVE TO YOU. DO NOT LET YOUR HEART BE TROUBLED, NOR LET IT BE FEARFUL."

Confession:

I thank you Lord that I have a sound mind, peace and love of God flowing through me each passing moment. No situation overwhelms my mind and my concentration is receiving the free flow of the love of God and the power of His grace shining through me to embrace my destiny. I see my way ahead and I understand every change of wind that blows around my decisions. Jesus is my decision maker and I carry out His direction.

I arrive at my destination knowing that no scale of any circumstance is bigger than the size of my God. I declare that I have a sound mind to make wise decisions concerning my life. I always end up victorious knowing that the voice of God speaks to my mind to lead me onto a fruitful end. I am able to make wise choices which allow me to enjoy life to the fullest without fear of any inner turmoil. Thank You father for blessing me with a spirit of "power and of love and of a sound mind" – 2 Timothy 1:7.

"I HAVE THE POWER TO CONQUER MY WEAKNESS."

24

Conquering Overeating

....

ood in itself is needed in life. However, one must not depend on food as the only source of living. Prayer and fasting are equally important and will help you out to see your future. The spirit of gluttony must be broken so that one can have a free

A PROPHET'S ADVICE - VOLUME 1

spirit to pray and receive answers to their prayers. Your body is the temple of the Lord and not the temple of food. Your passion must be to hear the voice of God and to hear right and enjoy freedom and bring peace to your life.

Breaking the curse of gluttony frees you to heal your body and become a living sacrifice, an acceptable offering onto God. You are not owned by food or possessed by gluttony.

Your satisfaction in life must not be based on food. It must be based on love and care. The spirit of gluttony must be defeated by bringing the human appetite and desires which do not glorify God, to order through a healthy lifestyle.

I now encourage you to meditate on these Bible verses:

PHILIPPIANS 4:13:
"I CAN DO ALL THINGS THROUGH HIM WHO STRENGTHENS ME."

ROMANS 13:14:
"BUT PUT ON THE LORD JESUS CHRIST, AND MAKE NO PROVISION FOR THE FLESH IN REGARD TO ITS LUSTS."

1 CORINTHIANS 9:27:
"BUT I DISCIPLINE MY BODY AND MAKE IT MY SLAVE, SO THAT, AFTER I HAVE PREACHED TO OTHERS, I MYSELF WILL NOT BE DISQUALIFIED."

114

LUKE 21:34:

"BE ON GUARD, SO THAT YOUR HEARTS WILL NOT BE WEIGHTED DOWN WITH DISSIPATION AND DRUNKENNESS AND THE WORRIES OF LIFE, AND THAT DAY WILL NOT COME ON YOU SUDDENLY LIKE A TRAP."

ROMANS 10:9-10:

"THAT IF YOU CONFESS WITH YOUR MOUTH JESUS AS LORD, AND BELIEVE IN YOUR HEART THAT GOD RAISED HIM FROM THE DEAD, YOU WILL BE SAVED; FOR WITH THE HEART A PERSON BELIEVES, RESULTING IN RIGHTEOUSNESS, AND WITH THE MOUTH HE CONFESSES, RESULTING IN SALVATION."

PHILIPPIANS 1:20:

"ACCORDING TO MY EARNEST EXPECTATION AND HOPE, THAT I WILL NOT BE PUT TO SHAME IN ANYTHING, BUT THAT WITH ALL BOLDNESS, CHRIST WILL EVEN NOW, AS ALWAYS, BE EXALTED IN MY BODY, WHETHER BY LIFE OR BY DEATH."

Confession:

I am an avenue of God's grace and I walk in abundance. I reject every spirit of gluttony that will try and control my life through the love of food. I ask for forgiveness for every opportunity that I have taken to be greedy when it comes to food and gluttony. Father, lead me to have a greater desire for foods that are healthy and clean for my body. For you said in your word that this body is your temple.
Help me to keep this temple that you have given me healthy,

clean and pure for your glory. Grant me the strength to be able to live a life free from greed, lust and piggishness. But instead help me to go along the road of generosity, clean thinking and obedience to your word. I thank you for your power over my life and I thank you that you are always by my side to bring me to success and joy in every area and aspect of my life. Glory be to your name.

"YOUR SATISFACTION IN LIFE MUST NOT BE BASED ON FOOD. IT MUST BE BASED ON LOVE AND CARE."

25

Legal Affairs

....

There are three levels of judges in the supernatural heavens: God the Father, God the Son and God the Holy Spirit. Where there is a dispute and disagreement in any situation, it requires a settlement and peace on both sides. Sometimes, it becomes difficult to settle without resorting to a higher authority. The secret is to forgive the other party, release them into the hands of God and take position to wait on the judge of the earth to rule to your favor. Bind every false witnesses, spirit of abominations, lying and accusation. Wherever there is disunity, there is chaos, confusion and delay. God is the ultimate and fairest of all judges.

Therefore, binding the strong man in the spirit, forgiving the physical person and releasing the case before God will always result in settlement to your favor. The Bible commands us to make peace before we go to court. Where it is not possible, the power of prayer and intercession must be strongly emphasized to bring peace and harmony in any case. The earthly court system is unsympathetic and only the winner takes it all. This breeds pain and resentment.

I now encourage you to meditate on these Bible verses:

JEREMIAH 33:3:
"CALL TO ME AND I WILL ANSWER YOU, AND I WILL TELL YOU GREAT AND MIGHTY THINGS, WHICH YOU DO NOT KNOW."

JEREMIAH 1:12:
"THEN THE LORD SAID TO ME, "YOU HAVE SEEN WELL, FOR I AM WATCHING OVER MY WORD TO PERFORM IT."

ISAIAH 43:26:
"PUT ME IN REMEMBRANCE, LET US ARGUE OUR CASE TOGETHER; STATE YOUR CAUSE, THAT YOU MAY BE PROVED RIGHT."

ISAIAH 54:17:

"NO WEAPON THAT IS FORMED AGAINST YOU WILL PROSPER; AND EVERY TONGUE THAT ACCUSES YOU IN JUDGMENT YOU WILL CONDEMN. THIS IS THE HERITAGE OF THE SERVANTS OF THE LORD, AND THEIR VINDICATION IS FROM ME," DECLARES THE LORD."

PROVERBS 14:25:

"A TRUTHFUL WITNESS SAVES LIVES, BUT HE WHO UTTERS LIES IS TREACHEROUS."

LUKE 2:52:

"AND JESUS KEPT INCREASING IN WISDOM AND STATURE, AND IN FAVOR WITH GOD AND MEN."

Confession:

Father, you alone are the true judge over all the earth. I present to you my legal matters that I am currently facing and I surrender them to you. Lord, take full control of the judge, jurors and the court system that will be trying my case. I ask Father for your favor in these issues with the law. Make me to triumph over my enemies in this case. Grant me your forgiveness in this case where I have gone wrong, and I ask for your mercy as this case is being tried in Jesus' name. Let there be a speedy and peaceful resolution to these disputes and help me to come out victorious in Jesus name I pray.

"SOMETIMES, IT BECOMES DIFFICULT TO SETTLE WITHOUT RESORTING TO A HIGHER AUTHORITY. THE SECRET IS TO FORGIVE THE OTHER PARTY, RELEASE THEM INTO THE HANDS OF GOD AND TAKE POSITION TO WAIT ON THE JUDGE OF THE EARTH TO RULE TO YOUR FAVOR."

26
Violence
By Fire

....

There are times in life when you must take possession of your inheritance by violence. Your enemy's job is to delay you and frustrate your plans. Every situation requires a different approach and consideration in arriving at a peaceful conclusion. You may have to result to violence by fire through the employment of the Holy Spirit's leadership, prayer and fasting as an instrument to conquer your enemies that is standing in your way of success. Situations in life sometimes demand peaceful negotiation but sometimes they require force to be applied if you are to win the war in your life.

We can only arrive in one of these two situations. One must identify the hidden place of the enemy, and target the weapons of warfare used by the enemy. You must investigate the enemy's weapons and locate the enemy's weak points. Violence of fire is your sure weapon for removing difficult mountains that stand before you.

This is one of the battles that will give you the head of the Goliath in your life, without which your enemy will rule your destiny, and control your dynasty.

I now encourage you to meditate on these Bible verses:

PSALM 56:9:
"THEN MY ENEMIES WILL TURN BACK IN THE DAY WHEN I CALL; THIS I KNOW, THAT GOD IS FOR ME."

ROMANS 8:31:
"WHAT THEN SHALL WE SAY TO THESE THINGS? IF GOD IS FOR US, WHO IS AGAINST US?"

PSALM 9:3:
"WHEN MY ENEMIES TURN BACK, THEY STUMBLE AND PERISH BEFORE YOU."

PSALM 41:11:
"BY THIS I KNOW THAT YOU ARE PLEASED WITH ME, BECAUSE MY ENEMY DOES NOT SHOUT IN TRIUMPH OVER ME."

PSALM 56:10:
"IN GOD, WHOSE WORD I PRAISE, IN THE LORD, WHOSE WORD I PRAISE,"

Confession:

Father God, let the teeth of my enemy over my life break. I render every aggressive altar impotent in the name of Jesus. Any covenant with the earth, surrounding my destiny, and every evil altar erected against me, be disengaged, broken and disgraced. Holy Spirt fire barricade my life from the rage of any satanic influences. I withdraw my name from every evil altar which is controlling the movement of my destiny.

Any sickness assigned to overtake my life, and withdraw me from my breakthrough, I release the blood of Jesus, on assignment to destroy the forces of wickedness. I withdraw anything representing me from any evil altar, or power crippling agents against my destiny be burned by fire. I release the wind of the Holy Spirit to bring every force of darkness allocated to my destiny to be destroyed by the Holy Fire of God. I shall not be a casualty of fire by the enemies weapons as the blood of Jesus covers my going forward and all my movements.

"YOU MUST INVESTIGATE THE ENEMY'S WEAPONS AND LOCATE THE ENEMY'S WEAK POINTS. VIOLENCE OF FIRE IS YOUR SURE WEAPON FOR REMOVING DIFFICULT MOUNTAINS THAT STAND BEFORE YOU."

27

Speedy
Promotion

....

Your altitude in life in every circumstance depends on your attitude. The heights you desire to achieve is always directly proportional to your prayer temperature. The airplane does not take off without preparing the engine. The same works for you if you desire to have a speedy promotion in your life. When you stay long in the realm of prayer, you will experience supernatural manifestation and exploits. You can always determine the speed at which you arrive at your destination. The choice is yours to fast track your promotion and make things happen beyond your human comprehension. The mystery of speedy promotion can be your experience if you accept that God is the source of all promotion.

Make a covenant to come into a relationship with God so that His goodness and mercy will always be at your disposal. All-sufficiency to your promotion is God. The resources to conquer forever remains the instrument of God's hand. It is not by might or by power in any circumstance of life. Cut a deal with God through the act of covenant and experience a supernatural promotion!

I now encourage you to meditate on these Bible verses:

PSALM 75:6:
"FOR NOT FROM THE EAST, NOR FROM THE WEST, NOR FROM THE DESERT COMES EXALTATION;"

ISAIAH 58:8:
"THEN YOUR LIGHT WILL BREAK OUT LIKE THE DAWN, AND OUR RECOVERY WILL SPEEDILY SPRING FORTH; AND YOUR RIGHTEOUSNESS WILL GO BEFORE YOU; THE GLORY OF THE LORD WILL BE YOUR REAR GUARD."

PSALM 3:3:

"BUT YOU, O LORD, ARE A SHIELD ABOUT ME, MY GLORY, AND THE ONE WHO LIFTS MY HEAD."

DANIEL 2:21:

"IT IS HE WHO CHANGES THE TIMES AND THE EPOCHS; HE REMOVES KINGS AND ESTABLISHES KINGS; HE GIVES WISDOM TO WISE MEN AND KNOWLEDGE TO MEN OF UNDERSTANDING."

ISAIAH 50:7:

"FOR THE LORD GOD HELPS ME, THEREFORE, I AM NOT DISGRACED; THEREFORE, I HAVE SET MY FACE LIKE FLINT, AND I KNOW THAT I WILL NOT BE ASHAMED."

Confession:

Oh Lord, I thank you for revealing your divine plan for my life and causing me to come into the destiny of your glorious blessings over my spirit, soul and body. I receive the supernatural empowerment for speedy breakthroughs over the work of my hands, and every other area of my life. I thank you for the anointing of excellence as it flows over my business and career path. I receive the surge of increase and multiplication to amass wealth and abundance. I glorify you for making me a Kingdom promoter and a Kingdom multiplier. Oh Lord, I ask you for wisdom and knowledge to do my job right and experience diligence in my business. Oh Lord, anoint the work of my hands for outstanding success and promotion which will result in praising your name and receiving my blessings for myself and my generation. I thank you for granting me supernatural favor before my boss, and anointing me to overcome every competition that I face to experience supernatural blessings. Oh Jehovah, thank you for making me a channel of supernatural blessings over my environment and granting me a life of miracle for supernatural, speedy promotion. I increase in all things that I do and I am called the champion of the Lord in all my endeavors.

28

Go Forward!

....

In every situation in life there are occasions
when one must decide whether to remain
the same, or go forward. If you choose
to stay the same, life will not be fun, but
ordinary. It's like a swimming pool: jumping
into the shallow end gives you little to no
fun at all. It is a place of safety, with little
risk in enjoying your swimming pleasures.

If you decide to jump into the deep end
of the pool, that's where the fun and the

reward of excitement is. One must decide to have a goal and a purpose to arrive at his destination. You must have the boldness to pursue your destiny with conviction and commitment. The passion to win must drive you to go forward. The glory is great as you march forward, knowing that the reward will also be great and fun.

There is a price to pay and a reward to be gained if only you are willing to pursue your goals with passion. As you go forward, there will be obstacles and other stumbling blocks, but the passion to win will push you to go forward and be declared the winner!

I now encourage you to meditate on these Bible verses:

DEUTERONOMY 28:13:
"THE LORD WILL MAKE YOU THE HEAD AND NOT THE TAIL, AND YOU ONLY WILL BE ABOVE, AND YOU WILL NOT BE UNDERNEATH, IF YOU LISTEN TO THE COMMANDMENTS OF THE LORD YOUR GOD, WHICH I CHARGE YOU TODAY, TO OBSERVE THEM CAREFULLY."

PROVERBS 21:1:
"THE KING'S HEART IS LIKE CHANNELS OF WATER IN THE HAND OF THE LORD; HE TURNS IT WHEREVER HE WISHES."

DEUTERONOMY 33:25-27:
"YOUR LOCKS WILL BE IRON AND BRONZE, AND ACCORDING TO YOUR DAYS, SO WILL YOUR LEISURELY WALK BE. "THERE IS NONE LIKE THE GOD OF

JESHURUN, WHO RIDES THE HEAVENS TO YOUR HELP, AND THROUGH THE SKIES IN HIS MAJESTY. "THE ETERNAL GOD IS A DWELLING PLACE, AND UNDERNEATH ARE THE EVERLASTING ARMS; AND HE DROVE OUT THE ENEMY FROM BEFORE YOU, AND SAID, 'DESTROY!'"

PSALM 75:6:
"FOR NOT FROM THE EAST, NOR FROM THE WEST, NOR FROM THE DESERT COMES EXALTATION;"

Confession:

In the name of Jesus, as I declare Your Word into my life, I receive the power in Your Word into my spirit, my soul and my body, in the name of Jesus. In my mouth is the power of life and death. I speak life into my life to energize me, to overtake and outrun my goals and become the winner. My heart is receptive to the promotion of God. My spirit is alert to the power of the Holy Spirit. Let the wind of your Spirit clear every obstacle out of my way as I triumphantly move forward into my destiny. I thank You Father that You have given me the power to be able to move from glory to glory, and strength to strength in Jesus name.
I take control of every circumstance that will try and hinder me from my going forward to the summit of my life. I thank you Father for the authority of Christ Jesus to break, damage, destroy and command every obstacle to be moved out of my way, allowing me to arrive at my purpose. I am led by the Holy Spirit to move Heaven to bring power

over earth and moves me faster to arrive at my target. I bind every power of delay, and I release "the go forward anointing" of the Holy Spirit to take over and possess my destiny. I declare in Jesus name I am a winner!

Conclusion

....

The greatest power and authority God gives human beings is an in-depth faith, and the confidence and the ability to move mountains of difficulties as we go through life. One cannot keep thinking about failure. As we work with God's established rules and principles, we are able to recreate our world and renew our strength to conquer any mountain that stands before us.

As we refuse to think and accept defeat, we are positioned to receive victory. Our attitude to winning and overcoming every void circumstance must be the ultimate goal and focus. One must formulate an objective, not a fuzzy, ambiguous goal, but that which is strident, specific and must be clearly defined. One must be willing to commit to pray and fast about the situation, have an inner conviction and picture that sink deep beyond our conscious mind. We must believe that God is able to sustain us and provide the in-depth strength to prevail and move our mountains and adverse circumstances to a successful end.

One of the greatest secrets to changing one's personality with respect to our problems is to enquire of the Lord the way forward through His word, the Bible. We must align our faith, confidence and trust in the Lord's wise counsel and wisdom in dealing with our circumstances. Many a time, the solution is right in front of us, but because we are far away from God, we tend to feel that God has abandoned us. He is always with us, in us, and around us in every way

Possible. We must never let any mistake or problem cause us to stop believing in God's mighty ability and skill to see us through to our destination. We must persist with total conviction that God is able to deal with all situations and circumstances. As we accept His leadership and guidance, we will always overcome and prevail in our locations.

Lastly, we must let God run our lives. He is the sure bet to victory. We must agree with God, and hence be at peace. Then success will become your inheritance. It is the will of God that we must walk in health, even as our soul prospers. May God bless you and provide you with an opportunity to successful life as you partner with Him and live according to His will.

"I DECLARE THAT YOU WILL WALK IN VICTORY AND POSSESS YOUR POSSESSIONS AS JESUS LEADS THE WAY. MAY GOD RICHLY BLESS YOU AND GRANT YOU FAVOR AND MERCY TO CONQUER ALL."

For more information:
www.tvineministries.org
www.vineyardprophetic.org
www.propheticflow.tv

Charles G. Gwira
Telephone: 416-477-1217
E-mail: pastor@tvineministries.org
Website: http://tvineministries.org